This Is What Made Me: Surviving Trauma, Challenging Systems, and Claiming Healing

Aisha Johnson Adams

TRIGGER WARNING

This memoir contains honest and unflinching explorations of trauma, systemic injustice, loss, and healing. Some passages discuss experiences of abuse, neglect, violence, and grief that may be difficult for some readers. Reader discretion is advised. You are encouraged to care for yourself and engage with this work at your own pace.

FOREWORD

The commonality we all share in life is ... the crossroads we come to. Those moments that demand a choice of how to navigate life's journey ahead.

How do we make the decisions that truly better our lives? Is it peace of mind, growth, security, honesty, purpose? No decision guarantees a smooth road. What matters is how we walk it. Even a wrong turn can lead to growth, to redirection, to becoming.

Sometimes your gut knows what your mind hasn't yet figured out. At other times, emotions cloud what logic sees clearly. Bring both to the table. Talk to those you trust—but don't outsource your life. You're the one living it. How will you feel about this decision later—proud, regretful, or, at peace?

In her latest book, "This Is What Made Me," Aisha Adams shares her life's journey with you. This is a strong and moving structure—a blend of raw honesty, strategic insight, and transformative healing. The metaphor of ingredients ("a tablespoon of pain," "a pinch of grit," "a tincture of reclamation") gives it a grounded, sensory, and soulful frame. It reads like a memoir-cookbook for survival, wholeness, and legacy.

This is not just a book. It's a mirror, a balm, and a map. Because we all have our journeys, our obstacles, our boundaries and our becomings.

This is what made Aisha. What makes you?

—Johnnie N. Grant, Publisher
The Urban News
http://theurbannews.com

CONTENTS

A NOTE TO THE READER

Hey y'all! Writing is the juiciest part of me, so you being here means I am becoming. Sometimes I linger too long in the prose, stack my metaphors high, and let transitions breathe. But I am always showing you more of myself. These creative nonfiction essays were written at the intersection of lived grief and a deep love for story. It's time to let some of it go, and I hope what I offer here will draw us closer.

INTRODUCTION

I wanted to call this book "Things I Didn't Think I Would Survive."

Honest, intriguing. At least to me. The first reactions came quickly: too sad, not hopeful enough. That stung. It made me wonder if my truth only had value when dressed in hope.

When my son Doriyan finished the first draft, he frowned.

"It's honest and not boring," he said. After a pause, "I guess I just realized, Mama, you had a tough life."

Maybe it's a trauma response, but I lean into difficulty; it excites me, and I do it well. Challenge has always been the prerequisite for the good stuff. Still, it feels good that my son wants something softer for me.

I learned love the hard way, and joy was even harder—fleeting, rarely central to the plot. Being a Black woman is complicated. We are judged in contests we never entered. Our feelings are runner-up to the grace, delight, and resilience we're expected to perform. Our brilliance always craved: Beyoncé speaks too country but not enough to sing it. Simone Biles is often penalized for being too good. That kind of scrutiny follows us into every arena, including these pages.

Rarely are we allowed to sit in the full complexity of our stories. Sit with me awhile. I've been carrying things, showing up, carving belonging in spaces that barely made room.

This is not a tea spill or a tidy lesson. Not a celebration of survival or a curated success story. You may not find comfort here. If you read this as a tragedy, you've misread it. Sadness alone will not save us. Without action, justice stays blind. Systems keep devouring us. We know we are delicious; they shake us, bake us, chew us up, and leave scraps behind.

What remains is a seasoned assortment of essays, wrapped in similes and warmed in reflection. These are the leftovers I'm willing to share.

Pass them around like a community potluck.

Each essay stands alone. Together, they trace my path through pain, grit, and reclamation. I live beyond these margins, but I've selected these as a mirror, a reckoning, a resource. Stir them into your conversations. Pour them into staff meetings, classrooms, and kitchen tables. Take what you need. Keep the jewels. Let what I've given be enough, even if you're still hungry when you finish.

I have been bent, broken, molded, and pruned into what you recognize today. This is what made me.

Now, how will you let this shape you?

This Is What Made Me: Surviving Trauma, Challenging Systems, and Claiming Healing

Aisha Johnson Adams

For Carly, Elle, and every young person still trying
to find their secret sauce.

THE THRONE: SITTING IN A TEASPOON of PAIN

Systems keep devouring us. We know we are delicious. They shake us, bake us, chew us up, and leave scraps behind.

If You've Never Been in a Hurricane

When Hurricane Helene swept through western North Carolina, she left parts of us gutted and our routines undone.

At 7:00 a.m., you stand at the door of Ingles in Brevard, exact change in hand, praying the pink poster's promise to open on time is true.

A man walks out with arms full of heavy bags of ice, sharing your worry about the power. Relief washes over your face. Finally, you will be able to flush the toilet.

"We can't sell you anything," the manager says, firm and detached, avoiding your eyes. "Our system is down."

You tell yourself it is not about race, but the guy with the ice was white. You know your Black skin makes you more visible, more vulnerable to judgment. Hurricanes do not play favorites, but systems always do. That is why Black and Brown communities are hit the hardest and recover last when disaster strikes.

Couldn't they jot down prices, use a calculator, take cash? But you cannot react, not in front of your girls, your niece and your new daughter. You will not feed the "angry Black woman" trope, though the Black woman in you is starving.

You imagine the worst: looting, families fighting to endure. The few businesses still open are cash only. ATMs are offline. Most places have closed.

Glancing back, you notice the girls have not said much. But they are sponges, soaking up everything you do and say. Your job now is to give them stability, even when there is none.

Leaving the store empty-handed, you try to convince your husband it is time to leave before things get worse. Maybe you can stay with his aunt or your mom.

He does not say it, but you know he does not want to leave. You feel the weight of the life you promised him.

"Power lines hang like Christmas garland," your new daughter blurts out. She is still adjusting, so you are happy she spoke up.

The sun is fully up now, revealing the damage. You turn left and see the guilty, musty, brown water where streets used to be, silent, admiring its work. On the right, homes are destroyed, their guts spilled into the street: broken mirrors, mismatched couch cushions, scattered mementos.

A school bus drifts through the muddy floodwater. Roads and bridges have been engulfed. You need to get to your son, but every route is blocked.

The towers are down, and calls will not go through. It has been twenty-four hours since you heard from him. He is grown, but still your baby. You have got to get to him.

"Why does the phone say 'Sauce'?" your niece asks, squinting at the screen.

You blink, then see it too. Not 5G. SOS. Save Our Souls.

Suddenly, you feel like you are the one drowning in fear. You force a smile for her sake, but your stomach twists.

A helicopter slices through the clouds overhead. "Yes," you say, trying to distract her, "they are here to help." You hope it calms her, but you need reassurance too.

You consider yourself lucky, even with two trees sprawled across the driveway.

After driving one hundred fifty miles through debris in search of gas or cell service, you finally catch a weak signal. A few texts push through.

Once you are reunited with your son, your chest loosens. You return your niece safely. You wish you could exhale, but there is still the matter of your new daughter. The one you promised the judge you would keep safe. You are not even safe.

The internet is back up, but there is still no electricity or clean water. Your phone feels like a lifeline as the death toll scrolls upward. In a small town, everyone on the list is somebody's cousin, coworker, or friend.

Outside, tempers flare. People jump medians, hoard supplies, argue in gas lines, and every need means a long wait. Rumors of a port strike stir panic. Toilet paper vanishes again.

By nightfall, a generator hums beside the house, part of the neighborhood chorus of helicopters and sirens. Every comfort seems to come with a price, either in amps or clean water.

You fill out FEMA forms, ration groceries, and try to keep the kids on a routine. The microwave needs too much, but the kids can charge their phones. That is something.

Taking guardianship of this little girl might be all the service you have left. You want to believe you did the right thing by trying to save her. But right now your life is shattered in mud and not just from the storm, but from the wreckage left by the systems that failed to protect her. The same ones that never properly served you.

They would have her for dessert.

Somebody has to stay.

Somebody has to love.

If you have never been in a hurricane, you may not know that the damage lingers, is thick, sticky, and impossible to avoid.

Your life was already changing, but now there is no way to go backwards. The storm made one thing clear: you are tethered together, whether you want to be or not, trusting love is enough to pull you through.

Son Shine

Doriyan is twenty-four now. This feels like tying up the loose ends of the fears I carried while raising him.

Doriyan was sitting next to me when I read the story on AL.com. The twins in the paper, Kenneth and Elie Miller. Young Black boys with their whole futures still ahead of them. Now one is dead, the other swallowed by the system. Kenneth had dreads like Doriyan's, though not thick and neat the way I keep my son's.

The paper said they ran. But I picture Kenneth turning back, expecting to see Elie, and instead finding him face down in the dirt. Kenneth is now being charged under Alabama's Felony Murder Rule with his brother's death, even though he did not pull the trigger. A trap. Now Kenneth must carry his brother's death and somehow not let it collapse him.

I feel for their mother, and for all the mothers whose loss gets etched in ink, laid out in black and white. The truth is, Kenneth did not shoot his brother. But it is still his fault. At eighteen, the part of his mind that could fully process this was not even formed.

I have been collecting these stories like passport stamps, posting them on my blog. Each one leaves a deep impression of injustice. Community trauma is subtle, heavy, and filling. It sticks to you like cornbread, and you do not even realize you have been carrying the weight of losses you never saw coming.

Before I could log off, another Alabama headline caught my eye.

Another set of young lives, gone.

I still cannot understand what would drive sixteen-year-old Jordan Johnson and his friend, fourteen-year-old Reynold "Ray Ray" Bonner III, to rob a man outside Lambs Mini-Mart. They should have known he would be armed and shoot. Ray Ray died in the hospital. Now Jordan faces charges under the same unforgiving law. Two more mothers grieving the loss of their boys.

I want to tell Doriyan. But there have been so many. I cannot risk desensitizing him. I cannot afford the "it-could-never-happen-to-me" attitude.

So I pick and choose.

We did the photo challenge, hoodie versus "good clothes," for Trayvon. He knows about the man shot trying to buy a rifle at Walmart. He watched me suffer through the details of Tamir's murder, a twelve-year-old boy gone in seconds for playing with a toy in the park.

It does not matter that he knows their names and can point out their killers.

He was raised to enunciate his speech, use polite phrases, and wear clean clothes because they are safer than name brands. And even though he knows his history, he knows he is American.

Do not confuse my teachings with contradiction, fear, or assimilation. They are strategies to keep us whole. If my son is ever erased, there will be no tropes. Only manifestos and legends about the angriest of Black women.

Tragedies like Kenneth and Elie's are not isolated. This is the reality for so many mothers.

Doriyan does not like sad son stories. When I try to tell him, he cuts me off.

"Why are you telling me this?" he snaps. "I'm good. You buy my food, my shoes. You're a sneakerhead. I'm fine. I don't need to know all this."

But I can always hear the fear behind his shrug.

He needs to believe my parenting can protect him. I wish it could.

Sometimes I cannot breathe, my heart racing, because of the sons I have taught who are no longer with us, like Devin Harvin and Octavius Boozier, haunting my hopes.

The line between life, death, and the system is so fragile. Close to the margins are warrants, court orders, and years that pull love until it frays. The Felony Murder Rule consumes the uninformed and leaves the rest of us living on edge. It is a system that could snatch any son.

I care about all of that. It deserves a petition, a protest. And so, I am writing this.

But my love for my son outweighs all of it.

So I tried to do all the things. I scraped together what I could, even when it was not enough. I showed up tired and burned out. I gave more than I ever thought I had.

I homeschooled him through middle school and pushed him through college. I taught him how to tackle, on the field and in life.

He earned an associate degree in psychology, then a bachelor's in health and wellness. His first job is in violence prevention, but his real work is my legacy.

He has never been arrested. He believes in God, family, and football. But it does not mean he is safe.

When I got pregnant, I did not know how to keep myself alive, let alone raise a son.

So we grew together.

I often served him undercooked noodles while he read my used textbooks aloud in our small kitchen, turning my inadequacy into a home with the little we had.

Our bedtime talks were about bias and boundaries. I poured in courage, love, and everything I had.

Even when the mix felt off, I kept pouring. I have not stopped.

Doriyan is not perfect. And some of that is my fault. But he is mine.

Calm like his stepdad. Sharp like me.

He plays games I do not like. He argues even when he knows he is wrong. Big-hearted, he gives the world too much credit, despite my protest.

These essays hold a lot of my struggles, but my happiness begins with him. Because in raising him, I got to rebuild myself.

I am sure the world does not owe him a future.

My son's life matters to me. But it has to matter more to him.

My duty is to make sure he grasps the weight of his existence in ways that those outside our experience may never need to comprehend.

He has to be strong enough not to take it, even when he is hungry.

He has to understand that running free in nice neighborhoods is not always an option.

Even a comfortable hoodie could make him a threat.

Because if he does not, this world will undo him. Without blinking, it will stomp him down like it did George. Or choke him out like it did Eric.

It has almost undone me too many times to count. But I am still here, still mixing, because I refuse to let it undo my son.

And Then There's Elle

I wrote this with the same urgency that Elle needs me, stripped down to only what matters. Each beat sharpened until it felt like walking a tightrope, every choice a test of whether I would fall or hold the truth.

When Raf bit his lip, I knew something else was off. This whole thing was already crazy, but I was mostly focused on Raf. I did not know what I was looking at. Compassion became my default.

For a moment, I thought Eric was going to die.

But Raf was staring at the shiny collar wrapped around Elle's neck.

"It's not our place to judge," Raf said, his eyes shifting toward her. "But we can't take her to work with that on."

My discomfort began to match his.

Later, Raf explained Rachel used to wear that collar proudly, a clear sign of submission to Eric. The only thing I know about human collars is that slaves were forced to wear them as punishment and were buried in them. Hers was weighty, titanium, with a key lock.

Seeing that collar on Elle made the whole mess feel worse. My compassion shifted instantly.

Eric had been known to show up in one luxury car after another, lying about Elle, pretending to be enlightened, probably trying to cover the ache of Rachel leaving him for his cellmate. Maybe it was the incarceration that got to him.

Seeing him filthy, naked, and mumbling beside the fire pit was unsettling but made sense. This is what happens when deception finally spills over.

My stomach flipped; the sharp, sour smell made me fear the worst. He had gone way too far with his daughter.

How far would he go with us? With me?

Raf had the best intentions, but watching him cater to Eric felt like he was choosing Eric over me. I felt the foundation of our marriage crack under the weight of it all.

I was scared and alone, even though he never left my side physically.

Eric sat on his back porch, frail and cross-legged, on one of Asheville's busiest streets. Rugs hung from the banister to block the view. A flickering fire separated him from us.

I could not help staring. I was judging him. The way he clung to control felt off.

This was not the Eric I first met.

He and Raf had been close friends for over twenty years. They held their friendship together through college, marriage, divorce, and prison. Raf wanted to believe loyalty could fix anything, even a man who had already failed his child.

"Honey, I'm going to have to ask you to take your mom's necklace off," Eric said, punctuating the moment by peeing into a glass while we stood stunned and unsure where to look.

I locked eyes with him because what if he could smell my fear.

"Your Uncle Raf says people might interpret it inappropriately," he added with sarcasm.

Elle whimpered, wrapping her slender fingers around the collar as if to protect it.

"It was my mother's," she said, small but steady.

"You don't have to give it back," I told her, stepping between her and the man who no longer felt like her father.

He could feel his power over her slipping, and she could feel my protection. Even Raf felt it, and he tried to pacify Eric by drying his sheets, mixing some strange drink with precision, and entertaining Eric's talk of leaving the country to get clean.

When I finally convinced everyone we needed to leave, we had space to breathe.

The drive home was quiet. What we had witnessed lingered in the air.

Grief, fear, and something raw sat between us.

This little white girl had been locked in that house for forty-five days in servitude to him.

No one came looking for her. Not her DSS social worker, who refused to engage even when we reached out by email. Not her middle school, despite her being absent three times over the truancy limit. And certainly not her mother, who opted out of her responsibility without facing any consequences.

If these institutions are willing to desert a white girl, what hope do the girls who look like me have?

A motherless girl feels unnatural to me. And now, here we are.

Because Raf was not careful, history looped back around, swallowed me whole, and made me a mammy. I knew there would be many more days, not just this Christmas Eve, when I would be forced to sacrifice for this family. This white family.

When we got home, I turned to Elle, malnourished, still wearing the collar.

"Do you know what a submission collar is?" I asked with as little emotion as possible.

"No, I don't," she said, annoyed, not at Eric, but at me.

I tried to understand where she was coming from, and I wanted to coddle her. But she deserved the truth.

She had been wearing it for years now in school and in pictures with friends online.

"Why do you think your mother took it off? Why was it the one thing she left behind?"

I knew Rachel took that collar off while Eric was incarcerated and ran toward a new life with new kids. By the looks of things, she did not give a second thought to her daughter.

Elle went quiet.

I could see grief, defiance, and a flicker of understanding on her face.

Then she whispered, "Good point."

I could not feel anything good or right about any of this.

Her hands shook as she reached for the key.

When the collar fell into her palm, she stared at it, unsure of what to do with its weight.

She rolled her eyes, crossed her arms, and turned away from me.

She was more embarrassed than hurt.

But something in her had shifted.

A few days later, I peeked into what was once my gym and now her room.

The collar was woven into a dreamcatcher, hanging beside a Whitney Houston Funko Pop.

It was proof that, for all she had been through, she was still just a kid.

I hope it catches the nightmares she's still too ashamed to share, and the lessons she hasn't yet found words for. But my hope is worn thin. Loving her through this is a fight, and I'm not sure I have rounds left.

When Love Kills

When I interviewed Falicia Blakely, who was convicted of murder and sentenced to three life terms, I recognized parts of myself in her story.

Watching *When Love Kills: The Falicia Blakely Story*, a made-for-TV movie about a woman serving three life sentences for a murder and robbery spree orchestrated by her pimp, was not enough. I could not leave her story where it ended. I saw her and I knew deep down it could have been me.

After the movie, I lay in my dark bedroom clutching my pearls, heart racing, grateful for how I had played the hand I was dealt. It took days to work up the nerve to reach out to Falicia. When I finally did, she replied within twenty-four hours through JPay, the system for communicating with people caught in the criminal justice system.

Before the murders, our lives mirrored each other like two tic-tac-toe boards waiting for someone to X us out. She was taken. I survived. Although we have never met face to face, I know her—not as a monster but as a sister, a woman who wanted only to be loved.

Our lives were symmetrical, our pain parallel. Falicia is three years younger than me. She had dropped out of high school before reuniting with her mother, around the same time I discovered my Mecca: Atlanta, a Black city alive with possibility.

I never lived there, but I loved it. Like the center square in a game of Knots and Crosses, Atlanta felt like the winning move. For Falicia, it was a fresh start with her mother. For me, it was an escape I could only visit, never fully claim. Since I could not afford to stay, I scraped up whatever I had and went as often as I could, taking diet pills to stay awake on long drives from Birmingham.

I imagined us wandering through Little Five Points, stepping into my favorite shops. I was eighteen when I first found the Bazaar, watching David Patterson build his world with tiny strokes. At Earthtones, Laneek's incense curled around me as I waited in line, her energy soothing my soul. Seeing Black creatives making a living off their art lit me up and made me believe I could be more even if I did not know how yet.

Falicia and I both breathed in the glitz and the glam. Atlanta dazzled. The difference was not desire but the fragile choices we made when the shine tarnished and the struggle set in.

Falicia started stripping as soon as Atlanta offered her fast money. I am not one to judge. I had my share of nights twerking at Vegas Knights, Club 50 Grand, and Bigelow's. I felt the rush of a Falcons win on my face. I had been inside a few strip clubs by the time she stepped onto the stage.

Atlanta strippers are stunning, perfectly nipped and tucked. They leave their problems on the stage in exchange for dollars. I could see Falicia stepping into that spotlight, elongating her body into a bow and arrow, skin shimmering, becoming the fantasy. I could never blame her for choosing to be adored, even if the end was tragic.

Atlanta is so shiny it either distracts or ignites you. Everything that glitters is not gold. I found the raw materials to build my dreams there. But at home the magic ran out, and I took what I could get.

I had been kicking it with a guy who lived two minutes from my community college. He was convenient.

For so many Black women, life is a tightly bound script with the same story but a different cast. We bend until our love stories break, and the trauma scatters like loose pages into broken homes.

Publisher's Note

This book is intended for informational and educational purposes only. The author and publisher disclaim any liability for personal or professional decisions made based on the contents herein.

Some names and identifying details have been changed to protect the privacy of individuals portrayed in this work. Any resemblance to actual persons, living or deceased, is purely coincidental or used with permission. The author asserts that all content is presented fairly and without intent to defame.

For permission requests, licensing inquiries, or rights information, please contact:

Aisha@aishaadamsmedia.com

Publisher
Aisha Adams Media
Mills River, North Carolina
AishaAdamsMedia.com

Praise for *This Is What Made Me*

"Aisha's writing can challenge your way of thinking about important topics in a way that is neither preachy nor judgmental. Instead, her writing is like that friend who only wants you to be the highest version of yourself."

—Javacia Harris-Bowser, founder of See Jane Write

"Aisha Johnson Adams is a talented writer. In her first essay collection, This Is What Made Me, Adams weaves a narrative of grief and resilience that showcases her thoughtful use of words to create art. Part historical document, part personal reflection, this is a book I will read again and again."

—Windy Lynn Harris, editor and author of
Writing & Selling Short Stories & Personal Essays
(Penguin Random House / Writer's Digest Books)

"Aisha Adams addresses life's challenges by sharing stories rooted in personal and community trauma, offering her truths with authenticity and vulnerability. Her insights extend beyond basic survival; they provide guidance for flourishing within a world marked by systemic bias and inequity. Her essays resonate deeply with readers, sparking reflection and reminding us that no matter what you have been through, you can still thrive!"

—Dr. Joseph L. Fox, Ed.D., MBA, PHR,
equity consultant, speaker, and educator.

When I told my son's father I was pregnant, he wanted nothing to do with me. Some children never see their fathers. My son has not, not once. That kind of rejection aches deep. It erodes your self-worth. The shame rots your senses. Nobody wins.

Falicia and I know what that shame feels like when a man leaves. The world blames the woman for staying, as if she should have known better. Men don't come with warning labels, and a man who abandons his own children can still find love and respect.

Michael wanted Falicia. Loneliness is a kind of boredom that can make what someone else wants feel like enough, even when they don't deserve you.

I shrank every time someone asked about Doriyan's dad, bracing for advice that was never kind. My embarrassment bloomed into shame, seeping into my psyche until I believed there could be no better version of myself.

I did not know what to do, but I knew I had to raise him. I wanted to. I left community college and went on to pursue my bachelor's degree. I got free counseling, wrote poems, cried a lot, and stopped visiting Atlanta.

I chose school while Falicia chose Michael.

My life could be read as texts and tests. I worked to love my life inside college-ruled lines. I built trust with my professors, spilled my guts at the school's counseling center, and finally tried to hear my mother's voice without resistance.

Michael taught her how to hit licks, then pushed her further. Stripping turned into prostitution, prostitution to robbery, robbery to murder.

He wrapped her in a storm of passion, fear, and control. He even put an actual padlock around her neck. In the end she was just another one of his girls. He called her Princess while her baby's father did not call at all. So she fell for it.

By the time Doriyan was two and I had settled into school life, I met the first man who made me feel like a woman again. Like Michael, he had a mean streak, though his control was quieter. I always tried to defuse him with jokes and ignored the red flags.

One reason it was so easy for him to trick me is because I have been around good men my whole life. I am a daddy's girl. My brother was my best friend growing up, and my uncles moonlighted as my heroes. I didn't know how to spot a man who meant me harm.

One night I drove his dark purple Chevy to a Chevron. A man at the next pump commented on my body. I smiled. It meant I was starting to find my post-baby self again.

But my date did not like it. He cursed so fiercely his whole body shook. While the gas dripped, I begged him not to cause a scene, not to pull his gun. I did not want anyone to die over my body. He gave me an earful for interfering.

I had to grow into the kind of woman who knows there is never a reason to beg the man you love not to pull a gun. Falicia didn't learn this lesson in time.

He never hit me, but I feared him and he knew it. When my car broke down he had it towed to his house. He waited in parking lots during my work breaks to see who I talked to. He did not sell women like Michael, but his charm bought him a subtler control.

I understand how easy it is to mistake attention for love. I let my need for affection blind me. These are lessons learned late, when you study a man more than you study yourself.

I dated a man who already had a wife. They were off when we met, but during our two years together they were on again too many times. I finally walked away. It was not easy, but I did it.

Sometimes I wonder if Falicia and I crossed paths at a CVS buying condoms or at IHOP sitting in booths across from each other, both with men who would never love us.

She headed to Blue Flame with Michael in the car, and I was on my way to The Fox Theatre with Mr. Manipulative.

This is not to justify Falicia's actions, and it is not my place to judge her punishment. But I feel connected to her. Her life feels like it could have been my alternate ending.

The only reason I am here is because, as my grandmother used to say, "God takes care of babies and fools." I have been both, letting love kill me softly.

The Scale: A Pinch of Grit to Balance the Weight

Community trauma is subtle, heavy, and filling. It sticks to you like cornbread, and you do not even realize you have been carrying the weight of losses you never saw coming.

Systemically Sidelined

I am going to keep showing up because some systems thrive in our absence.

When people complain about jury duty, my skin crawls. Chile, not me, skipping the chance to ensure justice for my community. I would never miss the opportunity to serve, not with everything we know about who this system fails.

Audre Lorde warned us, "The master's tools will never dismantle the master's house." But these are the only tools we have. Jury duty feels like a rusted nail holding up a house already rotting at the baseboards.

No one wants to serve in a rigged, dangerous system. Like voting, jury duty is a rusty tool, flawed but still one of the few ways we can raise our voices until we build something better. Still, I never want to miss a chance to bear witness, weigh in, and engage.

The last time I caught my mother trying to wiggle out of jury duty, she cut me off before I could even get started.

"Call Trump and see if he can let you swap places with me," she said, waving me off. "I'm getting a doctor's excuse. I don't care what you think of me."

I laughed at her sass but cringed inside. I know the wisdom she brings into every room.

Black women were not even allowed to serve on federal juries until 1957. I try to be gentle with my golden girl. Her resistance is rest, and she has earned the right to say no.

Mama's no is a protest, but my yes is a rebirth.

For Mama, jury duty is not civic engagement. It is one more interruption in a life already full of errands and care work. For me, it is an opportunity to engage. I will miss a little money and a lot of time, but it is worth it.

It is no secret. Even when we show up, the system finds ways to shut us out. Black jurors are struck down for their posture, their tone, even their attitude. This is not accidental oversight but a deliberate strategy to uphold systemic racism in the courts. By excluding Black voices from juries, the legal system ensures verdicts reflect the culture of white supremacy, continuing to deny justice to my communities. This practice perpetuates cycles of over-sentencing and shields injustice from accountability.

Bias is baked into the beams, but still, we hammer because silence will not save us. I stand on this soapbox so Sybrina Fulton can see me.

When Trayvon Martin's killer was not found guilty, I had to process my own anguish first. Then it was my job to stand in front of a classroom full of seventeen-year-old Black boys, trying to explain how justice does not always honor its promises to us.

Our community mourned. Some wore hoodies. Others marched. The young ones flooded social media with grief and fire.

What still haunts me about George Zimmerman's trial is this: there were six women. Not a single Black auntie, sister, or mama. No one with the lived experience to say that walking home in a hoodie, eating Skittles, is not suspicious. It is just a childhood. No one to argue that Black boys deserve to taste the rainbow and live long enough to spend the pot of gold at the end.

As matriarchs, we have to sit in the spaces our grandmothers were denied. The scales of justice have been tipped out of our favor for so long, it feels wrong to skip a summons. I understand that if I want justice, I have to come ready. Skirts hemmed. Heads high. Step over the debris and engage.

The system does not deserve us. But our people always do. That is why I always show up for jury duty.

Blurred Lines

I wanted to braid together the class lines I grew up with in Birmingham, Alabama, letting the truth split them clean down the middle.

Birmingham taught me the power of lines, when to stay behind them, what happens when they blur, and the penalty tax for dancing along the edges of those drawn to keep you out.

Birmingham, carved between parallel ridges at the edge of the Appalachians, was built for steel. The ridge drew a bold line separating wealth and opportunity from struggle. The city has changed a lot, but those class lines remain, only slightly perforated.

My parents were from the side where pollution settled. By the time I was born, legal segregation was over, but my mother never cared much about what was happening on the other side—not even when Target, Saks Fifth Avenue, or the new movie theater arrived. For most of my childhood, neither did I.

At sixteen, I got my driver's license and started exploring. I drove across the line to the Galleria and Target. My friends and I didn't talk about the divide, but we all wanted to cross it. We would sneak into suburban libraries to finish senior papers, standing in line to use the good copiers.

The summer after sophomore year, my best friend and I worked at department stores over the mountain. After work, she'd scoop me up in her burgundy car, and we'd ride through Mountain Brook and Greystone. We drove past brick castles with bay windows glowing like rap videos, driveways curling like cursive. She left inspired. I left aching, staring at a blueprint I could not afford. At $115,000 a year, it might as well have been another country, and I was just an English major collecting rejections. The line marked more than wealth. It decided who gained access to what, and whole lives were written off by which side they were born on.

Our side of the ridge had its own appeal. My mother's house pulsed with fish frying, cards slapping, kids tossing footballs, and dancing for dollars. You didn't see that over the mountain. It was the kind of fun that left a lived-in mess. Our side was alive.

I dated guys who said they could get me over the mountain. They had flash but came with court cases. They toed the line toward freedom and almost always lost.

When Corey vanished to life in prison for killing his best friend over money, I stopped pretending the danger did not touch me. I was in over my head, chasing dreams with men who couldn't outrun their pasts.

I decided I would make it over the mountain on my own.

It felt like a struggle, but I had a family-owned home, a support system, and a shot at a degree. When I started substitute teaching, I was stunned to learn how many of my students at Hayes High had never crossed the ridge.

Some had only been to the Galleria. None had seen the libraries, the schools, or the parks. They didn't know what they were missing.

My students shared everything with me, from their sexual identities to their medical diagnoses and even their quietest fears. They were ripe, raw, and exhausted. A few came out to me because they wanted me to know they felt safe. One girl let me call her by her middle name because it reminded her of the mama she had lost.

The mountain was my line, not theirs. Theirs was the line of survival, it was thin and jagged. That's why they pulled out phones in class, clapped back when my tone slipped, and questioned my grading system if it smelled like a setup. They were navigating real life—babies, homelessness, pain. Some problems were the same ones my twenty-something friends faced. Others, my friends and I could not begin to imagine.

In every class, a few were fighting court cases. They weren't criminals. They were just trying to get out, or at least through. Most didn't even realize they were trapped in a system designed to overstimulate and discard them over the tiniest infraction.

My students were painting a bigger picture for me, coloring outside the margins through persistence. They did not need saving— just a sharper lens and a steadier hand to teach the way.

When I graduated, I left Birmingham. I still visit. The line is still there, now perforated. I know which side made me, and I carry it with me everywhere I go.

Ways to Lose a Best Friend

There are many ways to lose a best friend, and not all of them are fair. Some endings come with a bang; others are snatched away without warning.

Cheryl: Losing a Friend Through Silence

Making friends in high school felt impossible. My clothes were wrong. My nose was big. Mama rarely let me get my hair done, so I kept it in a bun in case a fight broke out. In JROTC, we wore our uniforms to school, and the boys called me a monkey at least once a week. The girls treated me like I was invisible. Most of the time, I was there because I had to be, dreading the bullying and finding refuge in the library.

I thought the scales were finally tipping my way when I became friends with Cheryl. She came with an automatic friend group—girls who were cute, college bound, and looked like they belonged. For the first time, I was excited about going to school. I finally felt woven into the fabric of the day, looking forward to the tiniest things: sitting together at the lunch table, splitting candy, making weekend plans, and sharing inside jokes. Their laughter became my armor against teasing.

Cheryl insisted we go over the mountain to the library for better resources. She pushed me to apply for early college admission in eleventh grade. I knew I'd end up at community college, but I applied to three schools to fit in—and was surprised when I got in. She told me I was smart, and I believed her.

Cheryl felt more like a young aunt than a friend. She had a car and the freedom that came with it. But Wilma, my mama, was the ultimate decision maker. Even in my senior year, she said I was too young to visit colleges alone. Cheryl expected me to push back, and I wouldn't.

When I got pregnant and Doriyan's father wanted nothing to do with me, Cheryl did. She showed up every day, cared for me more than I did, and spent too much money on baby shower gifts. And that was when everything fell apart. I was grateful but so busy admiring her world that I forgot to live on my own. Neither of us understood that no amount of girl talk, gifts, or drinks could stitch up the gash of being unwanted by my baby's father. I needed therapy. I needed someone who could hold the heavy parts of me I was afraid to share.

One day I asked if she had read my blog. She laughed. "What's a blog?" I felt the distance between us stretch wider. Beyond childbirth, she had never been part of my story. I was always just listening to hers.

Our friendship was uneven. She liked feeling like I owed her something and collected it through emotional labor. And this went on for years until my gratitude collapsed under the weight of her expectations. I had nothing left to give. I didn't want to be in the dynamic anymore.

Mama said, "I thought that friendship had been over."

"All she does is piss you off," my husband retorted.

Pausing the friendship hurt.

No birthday greeting. No updates on her travels. No word on what happened with that guy. Not knowing made me woozy; I could barely stand it.

I was married with a child, but without Cheryl, I felt othered and alone. I missed her stories, her perspective, the way she made things make sense. Black women deserve sister friends with all the complications and softness they bring, but that is never a substitute for the healing that comes from a true therapeutic release. Things might have been different if I had gotten the help I needed sooner.

Since then, I have learned that silence is one of the gentler ways to lose a friend. Some best friends are stolen from the world and grief moves in to take their place. It is cumbersome and relentless. One day, you look up and realize you have carried that absence longer than you ever held the friend.

Losing Cheryl taught me how absence can hurt, but losing Goldie hollowed out my desire to connect. I didn't really even care to have another best friend.

Goldie: Losing a Friend for Good

I lost Goldie, a beautiful brown-skinned boy with a heart of gold lined in diamonds and pearls, to HIV/AIDS. He had a softness about him, even when the world tried to harden him. Where Cheryl made me feel like I was always trying to catch up, Goldie just wanted to play with me.

"Rock that 'fro," he would say, making me feel free and beautiful. "Shake them hips, girl." People who couldn't see the real Goldie, like his mama, thought he had a thing for me. Doriyan even asked once, "Is he my father?"35

Goldie had a wild side. He could not be faithful to his cute banker boyfriend, who had not fully come out. It hurt him, and he partied to withstand being stuffed in a closet he was too big for.

One night Mama, Goldie, and I waited in line for hours to see Erykah Badu live at the *Tom Joyner Morning Show*. We had worn her debut album Baduizm out. We talked for hours about human behavior and universal truths, thinking we were so evolved. I thought we were inseparable.

When I moved to D.C., we drifted. When I moved to Asheville, even more. Still, we would talk for hours when we could.

I heard about his diagnosis before he told me. By the time he was ready to talk, he was overwhelmed and wanted to convince himself I would be all right without him. The medicine wasn't easy on him. He said it felt like it was killing him.

He told me he wanted to meet my husband. So Raf and I met him at a record store on the Southside. I could not believe how frail he was, but I found comfort in him being proud of me for marrying a sensitive man. "That will help me rest easier," he said.

Loving Goldie was easy. I could just be myself. Losing him meant losing parts of myself I will never find. I wrote to him in Facebook Messenger for months after he was gone because I was not ready to let go. Eventually I had to.

I didn't think I had a heart left to break after Goldie was gone, and so I was devastated to learn a friendship could dissolve even when the love was still intact.

Raf: Losing a Friend in Love

I was shocked when Raf slipped away from me.

It was Christmas Eve, 2023. I was drinking my pre-workout, headed to the Raku Room, talking with Shawn. Then Eric asked one question that unraveled Raf: "If someone calls, will you vouch for my parenting?"

Raf always wants to see the best in people, sewing silver linings where there are none. This time, it was his best friend—the one who had been his roommate after college. On top of that was the shame of Raf never listening when I said, "I wouldn't be friends with someone who never has their kid. If they can turn their back on their own children, you can't trust them."

Raf couldn't yet grasp that no matter how tight you hold on, sometimes losing a best friend is inevitable. The sting he felt was grief for who Eric used to be. Blinded by love, Raf held on as tight as he could. But in not letting go, other things began to slip away.

I brought Elle home because she was in a bad situation. Raf brought her home out of obligation and guilt. They were both too broken to connect. So, with what little of me was left, I had to carry all three of us through.

Raf was in the house, but the window to our love felt sealed shut. I could barely breathe inside it.

"Hey, Elle has all of my damn spoons—the ones I saved up to buy from Dillard's—in her room. Go get them."

He ducked, dodged, or did whatever he could for a false sense of peace. I went a year without respite or protection. I wasn't sure if our marriage had run its course. Some days it felt like he had an "out to lunch" sign taped to his forehead.

His avoidance was suffocating because Raf has always been my launch pad and soft landing. Now, my fourteen spoons, three forks, and a bit of my dignity were buried at the bottom of Elle's closet.

Things went from bad to worse before I realized I could not fix it on my own.

Time taught me that a sensitive man needs a tender woman. Goldie never mentioned how hard it would be to soften to someone else's shortcomings to love them, but in his own way he showed me. Raf and I are finally unpacking our traumas together in therapy. I chose therapy over divorce because we have been good to and for each other.

The truth burns and leaves me chafed, but this marriage made me, and I will fight for it. Because saving us proves all loss is not permanent—and some best friends you do get to hold onto.

I've had my fair share of friends. I have more stories than I can count, and not enough of them have happy endings. Now I know how to choose, show up, and fight for the ones worth keeping. I have found ways to grieve those I will never get back. Most of all, I've learned how to love others without losing myself.

Friendships are a trip. Some are short, fantastic rides; others are long and winding roads. There are always detours, and certainly potholes. We grieve the roadblocks, the friends we lose along the way, and stay in our lanes for years, grateful for the love, however long it lasts.

I Didn't Like That About Myself

Sometimes I can't stand things about myself, so I drag them onto the page. I wrestle with them between paragraphs and edits until I make myself whole.

Like both of my parents, I am a workaholic. My mom still works three jobs, even though her children are grown and she doesn't have a mortgage. She is the go-to person for the overnight shift, even after a full day's work. My dad, a retired Marine, spends most of his time volunteering—leading mission work, prison ministry, deacon duties, and youth outreach.

In my family, your work ethic was never just about money. It was about purpose and perseverance.

"A man who doesn't work, doesn't eat. It's in the Bible," my dad always says.

My grandmother would add, "If they read one book, you better read two."

I grew up believing work was how we proved our worth as individuals and as Black people. As a kid, I listened to Dr. King's "Blueprint for Your Life" on repeat. His words burned into me:

"Even if it falls to you to be a street sweeper, sweep streets like Michelangelo painted pictures."

So I worked.

As a single mom on welfare, I finished college and earned a master's degree. I became a schoolteacher, then moved into nonprofit leadership. I endured dangerous-person drills, bomb threats, gang fights, and funerals. I said yes to overtime. I said no to rest.

When I launched my business, I doubled down, working eighty-hour weeks while homeschooling my teenager. I was proud of us. Exhausted, but proud.

Then my body broke.

On my fortieth birthday, fibroids so large I could barely walk bled for weeks. An irregular mammogram followed. Then a pelvic exam that left me uneasy for months. And finally, three blood clots in my leg.

I scheduled surgery between business trips. I launched an institute from the couch.

Two days after my hysterectomy, I was back at work, smiling through a television interview, uterus freshly removed.

I looked good.

But I was mad.

How had I become someone who showed up for everything except herself? Hustle culture doesn't teach us that when you are doing heart work, it is essential to put your body first, even though it's necessary.

I didn't like that about myself.

So I changed.

When I was well enough to stand, I got on the treadmill. Thirty minutes a day, even if broken into chunks. It was Black History Month, so I queued up Dr. King's speech again. This time, one line pierced me:

"Number one in your life's blueprint should be a deep belief in your own dignity, your worth, and your own somebodiness."

I had missed that part as a child.

I had been taught to always adapt, push through, but never to protect my dignity through rest. Never to admit my fragility.

So I had untangled that.

I let go of working through sickness like it was a badge of honor. I started setting boundaries. I said no. I chose slower days, deeper breaths, and moments to stretch my hips.

I am still a workhorse. My goals are high, from my physical training to my multi-six-figure business. But now I set goals around my rest and desires, too. Because if I want to show up fully, I have to be happy. Because if I want to do the work, I have to be here to do it.

Choosing rest has cost me. Friends. Opportunities.

I have had to trade contracts I wanted for the rest and rejuvenation I needed to keep showing up.

I have gotten better at what I do, and how I do it.

I have gained wisdom and wealth.

But more importantly, I now wake up daily knowing that resting is a radical act of self-love and also resistance. And I like myself more when I am rested.

A Tincture of Reclamation: Restoring Joy and Legacy

Living out my faith has helped me find inner peace, even when systems and people failed me.

No Trades

I studied to show myself approved. Then I put my hands, feet, and heart to work.

During a volunteer event, a white friend joked, "Okay, it's starting to feel like church in here. When I was a kid, I hated going to church. Especially white church. They don't have any fun."

I laughed. "Oh, I loved white church growing up. They had the best field trips."

He shot back, "I'll trade you all my white church for your Black church."

We laughed until we had to separate before people started turning toward us. But the joke stayed with me longer than I expected. Living out my faith has helped me find inner peace, even when systems and people failed me. Reclaiming my faith has been part of reclaiming myself.

Growing Up Baptist

I grew up in a small Black Baptist church that was more than a place of worship, it was the heart of our community.

Sunday School, choir practice, Vacation Bible School, and church anniversaries filled our days. Kids got free summer lunches there. Elders cast their votes. The sanctuary held us through good times and struggle.

Church was also about presentation and pride. I loved the polished patent leather shoes, the colorful dresses, and the older women in fascinators and fur who carried themselves with a grace I longed for. I wanted to grow into their dignity, their service, their faith.

Sunday School gave me my first taste of leadership. I lugged extra Bibles from home, collected offering money, and invited friends. Walking the aisle to collect our class's award banner made me feel useful and important.

It was there I learned to care for myself and others because we are all children of God.

Attending White Church

When my family moved across town, a set of popular twins whose father was an Episcopal pastor invited me to their youth group. I was curious.

Their church was nothing like mine. The pews smelled faintly of polished wood. The air was cool and still. There were only soft whispers, modest outfits, and music that felt restrained, but God was present and whispered a quiet lesson.

At first, I felt disconnected, almost invisible. But sitting in those neat rows, hearing the slow turning of Bible pages, I realized worship could be subtle and gentle too.

As a Black girl, I was taught to always be serving, through the choir, the usher board, or even my outfits. White church showed me I didn't have to perform or stand out to serve God.

It stretched me in ways I didn't expect and reminded me that God also listens to unspoken prayers and quiet gestures of the heart.

We went on field trips, played games, and studied our Bibles. It lacked the intimacy of my Baptist church, but it opened me to a truth I still carry: God meets us everywhere, even in our solitude.

Attending the Mosque

Curiosity about God kept pulling me farther from what I had been taught.

It eventually led me to Mosque No. 69. The Brother Minister and his wife were young, Black, and politically conscious.

I fell deep into the teachings of the Qur'an. I craved discipline and structure. It was easy to read but hard to live. I wanted a faith I could see and feel in my daily life, and I looked for it in the mosque.

Learning new customs was humbling. Modest dress, cleaner speech, and stricter music choices all felt like starting over.

I wasn't the best Muslimah. I never earned my X and never mastered "eating to live." The expectation to cook, clean, and raise children did not align with my dreams.

People often think Muslim women don't have a voice, that they hide behind their hijabs. But I wrote my first national article for *The Final Call*. My voice wasn't just present, it was published.

The Brother Minister and his wife guided me patiently. They taught me the mercy of Allah and reminded me how much God loves repentance.

Here, love was action. A verb. Not a performance. Through the beauty of the Nation of Islam, I learned that faith lives in motion, in bowed heads, in open hands, in choosing mercy again and again.

Do you give your change to the man on the corner?

Do you raise the child someone else walked away from?

That, too, is worship.

That is God's work.

Lessons and Growth

My journey is not over, but I am grateful to know that whether I serve from the front of the sanctuary or rest in the last pew, God's grace finds me in every season.

Black churches. White churches. Mosques. And beyond.

"For where two or three gather in my name, there am I with them." —Matthew 18:20

Every spiritual community I've encountered has shaped me for the better. They have taught me to use forgiveness, faith, empathy, patience, and love as daily tools.

For me, faith now looks like paying debts on time, keeping promises, giving my best, and meeting people where they are.

If my friend offered that trade again, I would smile and say:

No trade.

I am holding onto the church pew, the quiet hymn, and the prayer rug. Faith has very little to do with where you worship. It's who you love, how you serve, and whether you choose God every day.

Fit and Fat

Loving my body is a race I will never quit, even if society keeps changing the finish line.

I want to lie to you and say the reason I'm not a gym rat is sweat, but the truth is, it's because I am fat, people stare, and I sweat.

Sweat is the skin's version of urine, and on me, it's nothing like the fitness promos. There's no soft glisten on my skin. Instead, it stains my clothes, soaks the couch, and causes my hair edges to recede.

But I can't give up. This is a life-or-death situation. And yes, I'd like to look better in front of a camera.

When AARP featured my weight-loss journey, I panicked. I overtrained, spiked my cortisol, bloated, and worried. Please do not let me look like a frog swimming in Nutella in this national magazine. Plump and stuck.

And of course, I did.

I have always worried about how others see my body. My arms are like alien invaders. They have conquered my fashion choices and even how I pose in pictures. I want them to disappear.

That is why I like a classic, clean look with solid colors—fitted and with structure. Nothing that makes me look wider or rounder. I am doing the best I can with what I have. Still, my body has been the source of a lot of shame, so I work out at home.

The Raku room, named after my favorite Tyler Perry series, is my sanctuary. My equipment is always honest, revealing the best parts of me. I spend 25,000 minutes a year with them, and they have names because they are friends. My treadmill is The Highest because that incline will humble you. My bike is Tyrone because on that seat there is no pretending. The Rakudushi demand obedience.

I started working out while trying to lose weight, and I have. I am down about 70 pounds, and still medically obese.

The CDC recommends 150 minutes of moderate cardio a week, and most weeks I finish that before some people have their second cup of coffee.

Strength training has reshaped me some physically but most mentally. Romanian deadlifts help make me strong enough to carry my grief and my groceries. And I keep at it to stay strong enough to hold my future grandbabies.

Even on rest days, I challenge myself. I stretch. I do body rolls, Downward Dogs, and long, shaky planks. Most of the time I am trembling and feel ridiculous, but I press forward anyway.

I love long-form cardio. By the end, I feel like I tried to escape the Rakahdushi compound and barely made it out alive.

At one point, I was doing all the workouts and still running from myself. Nobody told me I could be fat, fit, and well. After 150 weeks of consistent movement and keeping the weight off, I am still a big girl. I had to force myself to stop chasing aesthetics.

When I sprint or lift in public, whether in the gym or at the park, it is like I am fishing because I catch the stares of strangers. Their eyes survey my curves as if I am for sale. In those moments, I feel trapped in an aquarium while strangers look in. My body becomes a spectacle on display, where their ideas about beauty, worth, and fitness play out—none of it written by me or even about me.

Skinny is what they think is normal. But I have learned their discomfort has nothing to do with who I am and everything to do with what they were taught to admire. The craving for a woman to always be desirable, is steeped in the poor taste of racism and the patriarchy.

Fatphobia is not simply a matter of personal preference or narrow beauty standards. It is an intolerance that threatens the health and well-being of entire communities, erodes trust in medical systems, and perpetuates systemic injustice. Where my weight falls on a scale constantly determines whether I am treated with dignity and receive proper care. Despite clear evidence that Black bodies do not conform to the confines of the BMI chart, my pain has often been dismissed.

Because I live in a plus-size body, I get the same looks whether I work out or let my body expand. There is no room for fat Black women in wellness, a space built for tiny white bodies. The clothes do not fit. The plans do not work. Fatphobia fuels a broader oppression rooted in the long history of Black bodies being commodified, exploited, and tightly controlled.

Doctors take the liberty to examine our bodies as if we are property, determine if we are fit to work, and deny us rest.

Loving my body is a daily practice. I have to work out in order to honor my strength and consistency, not to change my appearance. I had to learn how to eat better because I want to live longer. I weigh my food like a zookeeper prepping snacks for a hippo. It is my defense against the real killers of Black women—hypertension, diabetes, and high cholesterol.

Now I am finally under 200 pounds. The hardest part has been maintaining mental toughness—keeping the discipline to go when motivation is gone, knowing that I can't outwork the body I was born with, and that the real lie is thinking we can out-train genetics.

No matter how many reps I put in, mine will not look like hers. I have to work out consistently, understanding I may never get a six-pack or thigh gap, and remembering to be gentle with myself when I eat too many French fries.

I am learning to be okay with being fit and fat. I work out to build, not to shrink. All praises to the Rakhu; this body is already enough.

Sundiata's Smile

Old stories can have new endings. The 85-year-old former Black Panther was released from prison in May 2023.

In college, every time I received one of Sundiata's letters, I hugged it, pressing it close to my chest as if I were embracing him through the pages. Sometimes, I'd take a picture I'd printed at the library off my wall and place it on the nightstand next to my bed. He's standing against a portrait wall, wearing blue scrubs, his smile so bright it almost hides the reality of his situation. At 69, he had more muscles than wrinkles, signs of a life built on discipline and strength.

Our pen-pal relationship started during Black August, a month dedicated to remembering Black political prisoners, freedom fighters, and the legacy of Black resistance. I'd learned a bit about him through my studies.

Though we had never met in person, Sundiata's letters were special to me because they proved our histories were intertwined like a lazy eight.

Writing to him became my way of honoring his contributions to our collective freedom. In return, his responses opened a gateway to Black history and deepened my understanding of resistance.

In my mind, I imagined us sitting casually in a cozy café on the Southside of Birmingham, sharing stories and laughter over mugs of hot chocolate. But reality was bitter—we were separated by hundreds of miles, concrete, Plexiglas, and the cold formalities of visitor approvals.

I agonized over my first letter, drafting it 23 times. Eventually, I chose imperfection over silence—anything was better than not reaching out. I even took my time choosing a stamp, torn between commemorating the 1960 lunch counter sit-ins or the 1964 Voting Rights Act. I settled on the Voting Rights Act stamp, a small nod to the revolutionary work that defined Sundiata's life. That night, I mailed him two pictures, two poems, and a letter, hoping to bridge the distance between us.

His response came in a plain white envelope. His address was written in block letters in the corner, and the stamp—a small American flag—had been turned upside down, a quiet protest. Across the front, bold red ink declared:

MAILED FROM

U.S. PENITENTIARY

I opened the letter.

"Peace! Young Sista Aisha,

"I really got a KICK out of your 'statue of liberty' picture! ☺"

"Anyway, I got your poem In Search of Freedom, and you know I love it! It's da BOMB! ☺"

Every word danced off the page, smiley faces scattered throughout, just like in all his letters. Even though he was serving 30 years to life, his smile transcended the page, masking the pain and the prison that held him.

Before Sundiata joined the Harlem Black Panther Party in 1968, he was a mathematician. He graduated from Prairie View A&M College of Texas in 1956 with a degree in mathematics and worked for several computer firms. But his focus soon shifted to the pressing issues facing the Black community: housing, jobs, childcare, police brutality, and the epidemic of drugs devastating neighborhoods.

By 1969, his activism caught the attention of authorities. Sundiata was part of Computer People for Peace. They met at his apartment to discuss the intersection of technology and social justice. He, along with 13 others, was arrested in the infamous Panther 21 conspiracy case, accused of plotting to bomb public buildings in New York City.

Held without bail for two years, Sundiata faced a long, grueling trial. But when justice finally came, it was swift; he and the other Panther 21 members were acquitted in under two hours. It was a victory for the movement, but I couldn't help thinking about the time stolen from him. Even after his release, he continued to be harassed by law enforcement; it wasn't long before he found himself back behind bars.

When I finally gathered the courage to ask him what had happened, he wrote:

"There were lights and sirens. The pigs pulled us over. I was the oldest, so I got out. Assata was in the passenger seat, Zayid in the back. The trooper took my license and registration, then told me to stand with his partner while he checked the car. That's when the other officer pistol-whipped me, shouting to his partner, 'He's dirty!'

Suddenly, gunfire erupted. In the chaos, I ran. It took them two days to find me. When they arrested me, the troopers cut off my pants, leaving me in shorts. A gang of them dragged me through the woods, hitting me with their shotguns, whooping and hollering. They only slowed down when a crowd gathered to watch. I was arrested on May 2, 1973, and later sentenced to 30 years to life."

Even when he shared these harrowing details, stories of his confinement in a space smaller than what the SPCA recommends for caging a German shepherd, developing tuberculosis, or the restrictions on food and visitors, it was clear to me that Sundiata's smiley-faced letters were a rebellion against his circumstances.

"Pray for me; my daughter is pregnant; I love your book; and one day, I'm going to hear you perform your poetry ☺"

"Love ya & struggle,

Sundiata Acoli ☺"

Today, at 87 years old, Sundiata is finally free. Over the years, we lost touch, but Sundiata's smile still sticks with me. I'll never forget how, despite his body being confined behind those walls, he wrote to me from a place of inner freedom. His smile was a quiet act of resistance, a way of reclaiming his humanity. Even through years of systemic cruelty, he refused to let them strip him of his joy. His ability to make others smile in the face of so much suffering taught me a profound lesson in Black joy and resistance.

A smile echoes in the back of my mind during my hardest days. I've learned that even in the harshest conditions, we can find our own inner freedom.

Sundiata's story is my story, his letters a thread weaving through my understanding of endurance, love, and struggle.

Even now, when I face life's challenges, I remember his defiant smile, and it reminds me that joy, even in small doses, is a revolutionary act.

Niece: Passing Down

Jamaica Kincaid once tried to pass her jewels down to the girl in one breath. I tried that. But baddies need more room.

She sits on a pillow on the floor between my knees, and I part her hair with my fingers slicked in coconut and clove oil. The scent hangs in the air, sweet and sharp just like her. Her locks slip through my hands, heavier now. She is too old for beads, though I miss how they clicked like tiny applause when she walked. I promised your mother I would talk some sense into you. I close my eyes because aunties have to measure how thick to pour it all on.

I know you want to be a baddie. Don't let Instagram girlies trick you out of real joy because you don't know what's behind the camera or what they had to do to get there. Be happy for others, but don't let their shine blind you to your own. You are already bad enough. (I pause, tugging gently at a section of hair until you look.) Know when to be good, and follow the rules until it's time to break them. Before you go off, check your reflection: smooth your hair, align your actions with your values, and stay honest about your motives. Even good intentions can lead to trouble. Protect your peace the way you protect your edges, especially when he world will try to snatch it from you.

I pat her head, sealing in the oil.

Act your wage. I used to overwork and undervalue myself, which made it easier for others to do the same. Once, I built an entire program, was not paid well, and someone else took the credit. Black women have been devalued, underpaid, and under-promoted by design for centuries, so measure success in both dollars and dignity. Do not let them cap your worth. Pay what you owe and collect what is due. Good credit gives you options. Money and opportunity smell better than flowers or Chanel Number 9, and you deserve all four. Buy your own gifts so you never have to give them back. Believe in abundance.

I glance at your feet.

Girl, moisturize, I tell you. True baddies do not walk around with ashy ankles.

Operate in your gifts. Put people first by moving with love and integrity in everything you do. When you see someone struggling, help. One day the tables may turn. Give with grace, take help with gratitude, and remember we all play every position. Do not let a two-hour inconvenience ruin your whole day. It is better to have too much than to come up short feeding your tribe.

Character will take you higher. Bet on yourself. Self-love saved me, and now it is my privilege to hand you these jewels so you can sparkle too.

Life presents its challenges, and girls need mamas, aunties, and grandmothers, especially in a world that uses us up but rarely protects us. Do not play small. Trust yourself first. That way, when love comes, you give from wholeness, not from an insatiable hunger. This life will try to show you what you are made of. Add your own ingredients. And when the world feels heavy, remember the days I twisted your crown, filling it with warm oil and love from my bare hands, loving you no matter what you do or do not.

Her face is as shiny as her hair. She has my sister's eyes and my mama's nose.

Now go on, with your bad self, and wear these jewels like armor.

Living Like a Hippopotamus

I placed this piece here as a reminder that we don't always need to be pouring in. Pleasure belongs here too—in the pages, in my life, and in yours.

If spirit animals are real,
mine is the hippopotamus.
Not Lizzie,
my forever pick, the purple plastic one
who got replaced by Sweetie,
the blue version
in Hungry Hungry Hippos.
Losing her was a big deal.
Not so much a pygmy,
I mean a *Hippopotamus amphibius*.
We are both common,
thick skinned,
barrel bodied,
stout legged and heavy,
built for power.
I didn't know it back then,
but no one plays with a hippo.
You let us take up space.
Chill.
Keep it cool.

Run

and swim.

We don't bark.

But we bite.

We avoid people.

So we prefer night.

Under your gaze,

our image distorts,

bought and sold,

reduced to ignorant or angry,

through the lies the hunter reports.

They call us aggressive,

but actually,

we are just

fiercely protective.

Vulnerable.

Unconventionally beautiful.

We're loyal to our herd,

and tender with our young,

instinctively

keeping them safe,

sniffing out danger

in dung

from miles away.

There's always more to a hippo

than what meets the eye.

I can't deny

our similar quirks,

like the way my jaw droops

when I smirk.
I'm not the kind of woman
who collects cute little hippos.
It feels too much like betrayal.
No pink polka dot magnets
on the fridge.
Not one ceramic figurine.
Because
being left in solitude
is the hippopotamus's ultimate dream,
roaming fast and free
through the grassy green.
This Black woman is, too,
made of flesh and bone,
misunderstood,
frustrated.
Let us live,
unbothered,
unbound.
Just remember,
I'm living like a hippo
when you see me around town.

Hellbenders, Butterflies, and Rabbits

On hard days I can still hear my grandmother's voice in my head. God rest her soul. Her lessons were quick witted and layered with truth, easy to understand but hard to live by.

I remember her, or at least I think I do: the way she ate apples with a spoon, how she loved a cute dress, a fly hat, a high heel, and how she was never afraid to keep a gun close by. I can close my eyes and see her in the kitchen, smell the biscuits, watch her on the porch, or lying in her bed. I remember her soft gray curls being rolled after church. I have a few memories of her pushing a shopping cart at Foodworld, but never under a tree, near a lake, at a park, or by a ditch. Her absence from those spaces shaped both my access and my interests.

Maybe that is why I prefer nature at a distance: sunsets from a rooftop bar or from my patio door, watching the occasional white squirrel while pedaling on my indoor bike.

I am not the dirt-on-my-feet, wind-in-my-dreadlocks kind of woman. My husband, though, is a mountain man who loves to bike, hike, and name birds on sight. He wants us out in nature every chance we get, showing me things and talking with me about them.

This summer I did my best to plug in. I wandered with him, searching for a spark of connection. We went from town to town, from trail to trail, and stumbled upon a few glorious views. Along the way I met kind people and saw beautiful landscapes, but I never connected to them the way he does.

I was standing by the Tuckasegee River when I saw them: Pipevine Swallowtails with black wings washed in blue, bright with orange, their edges tipped in white. From a distance they looked delicate, almost unreal, like stained glass hovering above the water. I lifted my head, following their flight, and for a moment I imagined my grandmother with a magic wand. I felt like Princess Tiana, the world around me alive in unexpected ways. For the first time, I saw myself reflected in nature, belonging in the frame.

Nature has this thing about first glances. They are superficial, never enough. It constantly asks us to look again, closer, beyond what the eye first sees. My grandmother used to say, everything that looks good to you isn't always good for you.

The butterflies proved her right. Their dazzling patterns were not decoration but warnings, reminders to pay closer attention.

If you had asked me to choose a neighbor between the butterfly or the hellbender, the butterfly's garden would have been my first choice. Yet beauty fades quickly, while sustenance endures. The hellbender is a giant salamander, all wrinkles and folds, prehistoric in appearance. If you are not looking closely enough, you might miss its beauty. Yet it is gentle, and its presence means the stream is clean. It may not be beautiful to the eye, but it is good for the body and the soul, essential when you need clean water.

Nature does not respect feelings. It demands patience, attention, and wisdom from all of us. Just the other day I noticed two Eastern cottontails stretched out in a meadow beside my walking trail. I had passed that spot countless times and never seen them. Rabbits rarely travel far, so they had likely been there all along, hidden in the tall grass, perfectly camouflaged, belonging quietly in plain sight.

Butterfly, rabbit, hellbender: nature's teaching tools. Nature is a magnifying glass, just like my grandmother. And when I remember to look closer, the ordinary is made extraordinary, and I see myself and my grandmother reflected there too.

ACKNOWLEDGMENTS

They say it's risky to write a memoir in your 40s, but I've carried these stories long enough. These are the things I've chewed on, the places that spit me out, and the truths I couldn't swallow.

To my father, for reminding me my life is worth sharing, and that someone might need these words.

To my mother, you are the pan I bake in, the steady place where I rise.

To my siblings, I love you both, and I'm grateful I don't have to write essays about us.

To Rafrica, for stirring the writer in me, holding space for my process, and reminding me that the story and the storyteller are both a gift.

To Doriyan, you made me a mother, but your love made me brave. You held me together and pulled me apart when I needed it.

To my daughter, Lily, our lives sifted together, mixed by hand. Uneven in places, tender in others, still al dente around the edges, but we keep cooking. You refine me.

To Windy Lynn Harris, Dr. Joseph Fox, Joi Minor, Andy Reed, and Dan Mayer, your notes and encouragement carried me through the hardest drafts and heaviest days.

To my editors, Andy Reed, thank you for sharpening my work while protecting its heart.

To Erica Lewis, for your friendship, for designing my cover, and for engineering so many of my dreams.

And to you, the reader, thank you for being in community with me. Your attention is a gift. May this book make us all better.

ABOUT THE AUTHOR

Writer and influencer Aisha Johnson Adams is widely recognized for driving meaningful change in both entrepreneurial ecosystems and community transformation. Based in western North Carolina, she has empowered local entrepreneurs to turn ideas into successful ventures—whether through her work with Black Wall Street Asheville, where she co-developed the GATE program (Growing and Accelerating Through Entrepreneurship), or by providing over 500 hours of coaching through Mountain BizWorks.

Aisha has also played a vital role in community transformation, founding the Lenoir-Rhyne University Equity and Diversity Institute, a pioneering program that advanced collaboration and belonging across the region. Currently, she is passionate about training doulas through Sisters Caring for Sisters, an initiative that supports maternal health equity by empowering women to care for one another, strengthening families and communities from the ground up. Currently, Aisha focuses on providing trainings, workshops, and audits to leaders and organizations.

Aisha earned her bachelor's degree in English from the University of Alabama at Birmingham and holds a Master of Science in Adult Education. Her work has been recognized with awards including

The Tzedek Impact Award, The Martin Luther King Service Award, WomanUP's Women Entrepreneur Best in Business Award, and the Jane Renfroe Coach of the Year Award from Mountain BizWorks.

In addition to her consulting and coaching, Aisha hosts a daytime-style talk show addressing important community issues, and she manages "Nappy Thoughts," a personal blog followed by thousands on social media. She is a sought-after keynote speaker, workshop facilitator, and community leader dedicated to cultivating culture, belonging, and impact.

THESE ESSAYS IN COMMUNITY

These notes offer context on where selected pieces from this collection have appeared or been featured.

If You've Never Been in a Hurricane

Featured in "Come Hell or High Water" (2025), a community-led oral history project documenting the impact of Tropical Storm Helene. Includes an interview archived by Buncombe County Special Collections.

Blurred Lines Birmingham

Featured in "Southern Equality Studios" (2023), a Campaign for Southern Equality initiative uplifting LGBTQ+ and BIPOC voices through art and storytelling.

Like Falicia

Based on the life of Falicia Blakely. Draws from personal written correspondence with Falicia and others in 2017, offering insight into the complexity of their lives and choices. A fuller reflection appears at nappythoughts.com/falicia-blakely.

Living Like a Hippopotamus

A version of this poem was published in *North Carolina Bards Poetry Anthology 2025.*

Discussion and Teaching Guide for Book Clubs, Writers, and Classrooms

Discussion and Teaching Guide

Thank you for choosing *This Is What Made Me* for your club, class, or personal reflection.

These questions are designed to spark conversation, personal insight, and craft discussion. Whether you are meeting around a table, connecting online, or journaling on your own, take your time. Some questions are light, while others may challenge you. Share what feels true for you.

Facilitators and teachers: Select questions based on your group's goals. Begin with "Reflect and Share" to invite personal connections. Move to "Listen and Go Deeper" for group dialogue. Writers and students may focus on the "Craft and Style" section to explore how these essays were built.

If you are a book club of one, grab a journal and use these questions as writing prompts. Your reflections matter, too.

If your circle discusses the book, we would love to see it. Snap a photo and tag @AishaJohnsonAdams on Facebook, LinkedIn, or Instagram. Use the hashtag #WhatMadeMeBookClub.

Reflect and Share: Questions 1 to 8

Use these to begin with personal reactions. Share one takeaway with the full group.

- Which essay grabbed your attention first and why?

- What line or moment made you pause because it felt especially true, surprising, or uncomfortable?

- Which story felt closest to something you have lived or witnessed?

- Where did you find yourself laughing, smiling, or exhaling in relief?

- Which character in the book stayed on your mind after you finished reading and why?

- What does being "fit" or "fat" mean to you after reading this book?

- From Niece, which piece of advice felt the most personal to you? What rule or life lesson would you add or take away?

- The dedication speaks to people still searching for their "secret sauce." What is in your sauce?

Listen and Go Deeper: Questions 9 to 16

These invite thoughtful conversation. Take turns speaking and listening.

- "A Note to the Reader" rejects pity and calls for truth-telling. How did that shape the way you read the book?

- What do these essays reveal about the cost of caring for others, whether children, friends, or strangers? Do you agree with the author's perspective?

- Where did you see grit show up the most? Which kind of grit (mental, emotional, or physical) do you relate to?

- What does reclamation mean to you? Where are you taking something back or making it your own?

- The author asks, "Will this be enough?" Where in your own life have you asked that question?

- Where do you see an opportunity to show up differently in your own community after reading this book?

- What does balance look like for you in this season of life? What strategies help you hold it?

- Which image stayed with you the longest and why?

Expand and Apply: Questions 17 to 20

U se these questions to move toward action or deeper personal reflection.

- Which essay made you think differently about love, friendship, or family?

- What joy-filled or tender moment in the book reminded you of something in your own life?

- What conversation would you love to have with others after reading this book?

- If you could give this book to one person, who would it be and what would you hope they take away from it?

For Writers: Craft and Style Questions 21 to 25

I f you are curious about how this book was built, or you are a writer yourself, these questions are for you.

- Where were you most pulled into the action and where did reflection deepen the story? How did that balance shape your connection to the narrator?

- The author uses storms, food, and bodies as metaphors. Which image felt the most powerful to you and how did it expand the meaning of the story?

- How does the author shift between being in the moment as a younger self and looking back as an older, wiser narrator? Where does this distance feel intentional and how does it change your understanding of the events?

- The essays move through grief, grit, and reclamation. How do shifts in tone including humor, anger, and tenderness guide the reader through those stages?

- The essays stand alone but form a larger story when read together. How does the grouping of Pain, Grit, and Reclamation shape your experience of the book? Would any essay feel different in another section?

Journal Prompts for Workshops or Personal Writing

Use these prompts for journaling, writing groups, or classroom assignments. Write for 10 to 20 minutes without stopping and share only if you choose.

- Grit and Reclamation: Write about a time when you had to show grit or reclaim part of yourself. Use one strong image or metaphor, as the author does with storms, food, or hippos, to carry the weight of your story.

- Friendship and Loss: Think of a friendship that changed or ended. What unspoken truths or emotional labor shaped that shift? Write about the moment you knew the friendship would never be the same.

- Rest and Healing: Describe a time when you chose rest even when the world expected you to keep going. How did it feel in your body? What did you learn about yourself?

- Your Secret Sauce: The dedication speaks to people still searching for their "secret sauce." Write about what makes you, you. List the ingredients of your secret sauce including traits, habits, or life lessons, and how you earned them.

- A Turning Point: Write about a moment when you made a choice that changed your life. What pushed you to make that decision and how did it shape who you are now?

Additional Support and Resources

I am available for Question & Answer sessions, guest facilitation, or speaking engagements to support your group's journey with *This Is What Made Me.*

Please feel free to reach out directly to me at Aisha@aishaadamsmedia. com to schedule a session or ask any questions.

For more resources including discussion guides, event ideas, and updates, please visit my website:

AishaAdamsMedia.com

We would love to see your group in action. If you share photos or stories from your discussions or events on social media, please tag me:

@AishaJohnsonAdams on Facebook, LinkedIn, and Instagram

Use the hashtag #WhatMadeMeBookClub so we can celebrate your community and conversations together.

Thank you for being part of this journey.

Soil Notes

These notes provide deeper context, sources, and personal reflections to accompany the essays in *This Is What Made Me*. Think of them as the fertile ground beneath the surface, where I first dug, questioned, and wrestled before finding clarity. They are the nourishing soil that fed the roots of my understanding.

I invite you to use these notes as a guide for further exploration, especially during moments when you feel discomfort or pause. These are the moments when growth happens, when the soil is richest and the seeds can take hold.

This is not a bibliography or a fact-checking exercise. I have nothing to prove. This is my diet, the substance I uncovered as I sifted through my story, history, and lived experience. It is what I have been reading, consuming, thinking, and living. Use these notes as insights, extended reading, or source material—or don't. It really is up to you.

As you read, I encourage you to lean into your own soil: your history, your challenges, your questions. May these notes inspire you to dig deeper, challenge what you thought you knew, and nurture your own growth and reclamation.

This is the soil that made me. Use it to fertilize your own abundance.

A Note to the Reader

Food as Metaphor

Food nourishes us, but it carries so much more: feeling, memory, even desire. In this book, I use recipes, measurements, and ingredients as metaphors for erotic experiences both painful and joyful. The act of mixing and measuring becomes a way for me to reckon with life's complexities and claim agency over what I have consumed physically and emotionally.

Audre Lorde reminds us that we have been conditioned to fear the "yes" within ourselves—the deepest cravings that connect us to our power and pleasure. In Uses of the Erotic: The Erotic as Power (1978), she teaches that embracing desire is a radical act of self-love and resistance in all that we do. This memoir is my permission slip to savor my cravings, truth, belonging, and the freedom to write. It is also an invitation for you to taste your own deepest "yes."

Source: Audre Lorde, *Uses of the Erotic: The Erotic as Power*

MICHAEL

Killer Mike's *MICHAEL*, winner of the 2024 Grammy for Best Rap Album, was deeply inspirational in terms of blending my journalistic side with my love for metaphor and memoir. The storytelling is unflinching, rooted in both confession and community history, it reminded me that truth can be both reported and performed.

Source: Killer Mike, *MICHAEL*

If You've Never Been in a Hurricane

"Disaster Does Not Discriminate, But Recovery Does"

Storms may hit everyone, but the aftermath is not equal. Black families are more likely to live in flood zones, less likely to be insured, and slower to receive emergency aid. This is not just about weather, but also about policy.

Source: NAACP Legal Defense Fund (2021); Brentin Mock, "Race, Place, and Environmental Justice After Hurricane Katrina"

"Relief Is Not Always a Rescue"

Even in crisis, Black survivors often face suspicion instead of support. They are accused of looting when gathering supplies and dismissed when asking for help. The trauma of the storm is compounded by the trauma of being disbelieved.

Source: *The Atlantic*, "The Unequal Burden of Disaster" (2020); NPR Code Switch, "Race and Relief" (2017)

Son Shine

"The Felony Murder Rule Disproportionately Affects Black and Brown Communities"

In Alabama, any person involved in a felony can be charged with murder if someone dies during the commission of that crime, even if they did not directly cause the death. This sweeping law has affected countless young people, women, and bystanders with life-altering prosecutions.

Source: Alabama Code § 13A-6-2

"Teen Brains Are Still Developing"

The prefrontal cortex, responsible for judgment, decision-making, and impulse control, continues to mature into the mid-twenties. This neuroscience shapes debates about youth sentencing and criminal responsibility.

Source: National Institute of Mental Health, "The Teen Brain: 7 Things to Know" (2021)

Their Names Frame Our Fear

Philando Castile, Eric Garner, John Crawford III, Trayvon Martin, Tamir Rice, Ahmaud Arbery, and George Floyd were unarmed Black men whose deaths sparked global uprisings against systemic racism. Their legacies reshape how many people parent, protest, and protect.

Source: Ohio State University Libraries, "Say Their Names: A Guide to Commemorating Black Lives Lost"

And Then There's Elle

Trauma Does Not Always Speak, It Shows

Children express trauma through behavior, attachment to objects, silence, or defiance. Such signals demand compassion, boundaries, and belief in their right to safety.

Source: Bessel van der Kolk, *The Body Keeps the Score* (2014)

Healing Leaves Evidence

Survivors often reclaim objects meant to harm them, transforming symbols of pain into artifacts of power.

Source: Resmaa Menakem, *My Grandmother's Hands* (2017)

Like Falicia

Art as Testimony and Survival

Ntozake Shange's *For Colored Girls Who Have Considered Suicide / When the Rainbow Is Enuf* gave voice to the pain, resilience, and complexity of Black womanhood. Like Falicia's story, it confronts the intersections of love, violence, and survival with raw honesty, showing that telling our stories is an act of resistance.

Source: Ntozake Shange (1975)

Creative Loafing Feature

Creative Loafing's two-part cover story, "Learning to Hit a Lick," dives deep into Falicia Blakely's life from her early grooming by an older pimp to the tragic violence that followed. The piece is vivid, unflinching, and empathetic, offering context that shaped my reflections on her story's complexity.

Source: *Creative Loafing*

Nappy Thoughts Interview

In 2017, I spoke directly with Falicia, her accomplice Ameshia "Pumpkin" Ervin, and their pimp, Michael Berry. These interviews uncovered layers of human experience including remorse, survival, shared pain, and the force of storytelling as reclamation. They also coincided with the year her story was retold on national television, allowing me to compare lived truth with dramatized version.

Source: Nappy Thoughts (2017)

Film Adaptation: When Love Kills

The TV One movie *When Love Kills: The Falicia Blakely Story* dramatizes her life and crimes, offering a stylized version of events that reached a national audience. While the film brought visibility to her case, it also highlights how entertainment media can alter or sensationalize true events for dramatic effect.

Source: TV One

Our Voice

Our Voice is a local Asheville, NC, agency that provides counseling, advocacy, and education for survivors of sexual violence. They remind us how essential survivor-centered care is in reclaiming voice and agency.

Source: Our Voice, Asheville, NC

Research and Understanding Trafficking

I needed a full understanding of how people are trafficked, how force, fraud, or coercion are used to exploit individuals into labor or commercial sex, and how victims often do not recognize themselves as victims. Deepening my awareness shaped how I held space for Falicia's story with nuance and care.

Source: U.S. Department of Homeland Security
Blue Campaign

Systemically Sidelined

Jury Duty as Civic Power

Jury duty is more than an obligation — it is a tool for justice. Diverse juries help ensure fair trials and better reflect the communities they serve. When we show up, we disrupt the tendency for courtrooms to be filled with people who look nothing like the accused.

Source: American Bar Association,
"The Importance of Jury Diversity" (2019)

Barriers to Participation

Work obligations, childcare, transportation issues, and mistrust of the justice system keep many people—particularly people of color—from serving. Addressing these barriers is essential for representation.

Source: Brennan Center for Justice
"Fair Jury Project" (2020)

Blurred Lines Birmingham

Historical Amnesia in the South

Birmingham's history is heavy with segregation, police violence, and community resistance. Yet much of that truth is absent in tourist marketing and civic branding, leaving an incomplete public memory.

Source: Horace Huntley & David Montgomery
*Foot Soldiers for Democracy: The Men, Women, and Children
of the Birmingham Civil Rights Movement* (2009)

Personal Witness and Place

Walking the streets where historic protests unfolded forces a confrontation with the ways history lives on—not just in plaques, but in poverty, policing, and power.

Source: Birmingham Civil Rights Institute archives

Ways to Lose a Best Friend

Friendship Breakups Leave Scars Too

Ending a friendship can be as painful and formative as the end of a romantic relationship. Whether through silence, death, or rupture, each loss reshapes how we love and trust.

Source: *Psychology Today*, "When Friendships End" (2018)

Grief Has Many Forms

The death of a close friend disrupts more than your social circle; it alters your memory landscape, coloring places, dates, and even your sense of time.

Source: Megan Devine, *It's OK That You're Not OK* (2017)

I Didn't Like That About Myself

Work as Worth

Many of us inherit the belief that our value is measured in our output. For Black families, especially, work ethic has been a shield and a proof of dignity in the face of systemic doubt.

Source: Martin Luther King Jr.
"Blueprint for Your Life" speech (1967)

Breaking Patterns

Choosing rest is a radical act when your identity is tied to constant productivity. It takes unlearning generations of conditioning to see rest as a right, not a reward.

Source: Tricia Hersey, *Rest Is Resistance* (2022)

No Trades for Me: My Journey to Faith in Action

Faith in Motion

Faith does not only live in words or in worship spaces; it lives in the way we treat each other every day. Acts of love, service, and solidarity are the truest forms of devotion.

Mosque No. 69

My visits to Mosque No. 69 revealed a community committed to political consciousness, self-sufficiency, and collective care. This space was as much about action as it was about prayer.

Source: Nation of Islam archives

Muhammad: A Story of the Last Prophet

Deepak Chopra's historical novel explores the life of the Prophet Muhammad through a unique chorus of voices from friends, enemies, family members, and allies. By choosing fiction over biography, Chopra unsettles cultural assumptions and invites empathetic engagement. The book encourages readers, especially in the West, to move beyond stereotypes and toward understanding. This book reminds me that writing can break down walls.

Source: Deepak Chopra, *Muhammad: A Story of the Last Prophet* (2010)

Fit and Fat

Rejecting the Weight-Centered Model

BMI is a limited measure of health. Fatphobia warps how we view fitness, reducing it to weight loss rather than strength, mobility, and joy.

Source: Centers for Disease Control and Prevention; *Journal of Obesity* (2016); Roxane Gay, *Hunger: A Memoir of (My) Body*

Peloton as Community

Online fitness spaces like Peloton can offer connection, competition, and encouragement, creating accountability without the shame often found in gyms. My leader board name is #NappyThoughts; join me.

Source: Peloton Digital Community Forums

Tyler Perry's Ruthless

Tyler Perry's *Ruthless* offers a raw portrayal of trauma, survival, and the complexities of life on a compound as part of a cult. The show's drama and layered characters inspired me to name my gym equipment after them because working out can be just as intense.   Source: Tyler Perry's *Ruthless* (BET+)

Sundiata's Smile

Black August

Black August is a month of remembrance and resistance, honoring political prisoners, freedom fighters, and the struggle for Black liberation. It calls us to study, reflect, and act in the spirit of those who came before us.

Source: Malcolm X Grassroots Movement for Self-Determination is where I learned the meaning of Black August.

Introduction to Black Studies

Maulana Karenga's *Introduction to Black Studies* lays out the foundations of African American history, culture, and liberation movements. It examines the political and cultural frameworks that shaped organizations like the Black Panther Party and the broader struggle for Black self-determination. Reading this work alongside Sundiata Acoli's story deepens the understanding of his activism, situating his life and imprisonment within a continuum of resistance and community responsibility. Reading this book made it easy for me to connect with Acoli and see his activism as a gift.

Source: Maulana Karenga, *Introduction to Black Studies* (8th ed.)

Niece

Kinship as Care

Aunties, nieces, and chosen family members often form bonds as strong as—and sometimes stronger than—those of parents and children. These relationships are spaces of mentorship, joy, and mutual growth.

Source: bell hooks, *Sisters of the Yam: Black Women and Self-Recovery* (1993)

Living Like a Hippopotamus

The Hippo as Metaphor

Hippos are often underestimated—dismissed as slow, ungraceful, or unworthy of admiration. In reality, they are strong, territorial, and unbothered by outside opinions. Living like a hippo means reclaiming your own body, space, and worth without seeking permission.

The Skin I'm In

Sharon G. Flake's *The Skin I'm In* is a powerful reminder to love myself in the body I have. That book showed me how deep the roots of ridicule can grow and how heavy it is to carry someone else's shame. Writing "Living Like a Hippopotamus" was my way of putting that weight down.

Source: Sharon G. Flake, *The Skin I'm In* (1998)

Afterword

If these pages have stirred something in you, let it be the start of your work. Show up for your people. Guard your joy. Refuse to be devoured.

The system may starve us, but our soil is rich, and everything we need to grow each other is already here.

Aisha Adams

Navigate Change
Empower Teams
Create Sustainable
Impact

Navigate Change with Confidence.
Organizations face constant transitions—
whether it's growth, restructuring, or succession.
The right support can mean the difference
between disruption and lasting success.

Services include
- Coaching,
- Consulting,
- Interim executive leadership,
- Facilitation, and
- Corporate training

With expert guidance, your organization can overcome challenges, unlock potential, and move forward with clarity and confidence.

aishajohnsonadams.com

SELF-DISCOVERY PROMPT CARDS

ORDER NOW!

30 journal prompts to build healthy habits

- Engage others
- Journal
- 30-day challenge!

4 CATEGORIES TO GUIDE YOUR PATH TO DISCOVERY

Boundaries

Character

Confidence

Resilience